SO-AZJ-909

<u>*Comments*</u>

The Search for Significance should be read by every
Christian.
Billy Graham

Your book is changing my thinking and has given me
hope. I am able to truly feel in my heart and not just
have a knowledge in my head of God's love for me.
Montana

Even though I had a relationship with the Lord for
many years prior to reading your book, all the false-
hoods that I grew up with made it very difficult for my
union to grow. Thank you for this wonderful, refreshing perspective on life.
Canada

The Search for Significance provides the answers I've
been looking for in secular 12-step programs and
counseling but couldn't find.
Houston

Our small group has found *The Search for Significance* inspirational and life-changing. The probing of the Holy Spirit through this joint venture has been evident in all our lives, and none of us are the same as we were when we began "our trip in."
Tennessee

I have been going to church and Sunday school all my life and trusted Christ at the age of nine. It wasn't until I read *Search for Significance* that I finally understood the impact of what it really means to be fully loved and completely forgiven in Christ. It changed my whole outlook about my Christian walk. All of Rapha Resources books can have the same impact—they are so easy to understand and profoundly practical in daily application.
Layperson

Even though I had a relationship with the Lord for many years prior to reading your book, all the false-hoods that I grew up with made it very difficult for my union to grow. Thank you for this wonderful, refreshing perspective on life.
Canada

Excerpts from

THE SEARCH FOR SIGNIFICANCE

BOOK & WORKBOOK

Robert S. McGee

Second Edition

Rapha
PUBLISHING

Houston, Texas

The Search for Significance (Condensed Edition)
by Robert S. McGee

Condensed Edition © 1994 by Robert S. McGee

All rights reserved. No portion of this publication may be used in any form
without written permission of the author, with the exception of brief
excerpts in magazine articles, reviews, etc.

Unless otherwise indicated, Scripture references in this volume are from the
New American Standard Bible, copyright The Lockman Foundation, 1960,
1962, 1963, 1968, 1971, 1972, 1975, 1977.

Portions of *The Search for Significance* book and workbook reprinted and
adapted by permission. Robert S. McGee. (2nd ed. © 1990 by Robert S.
McGee; Houston and Dallas, TX: Rapha Publishing/Word, Inc.)

First Printing, 1994
Printed in the United States of America
ISBN: 0-945276-53-2

CONTENTS

NOTE. The bolded text above indicates the contents of this condensed version of *The Search for Significance*. The following chapters and workbook steps indicate additional text available in the original book/workbook version.

THE SEARCH FOR SIGNIFICANCE WORKBOOK

INTRODUCTION

When Christ told His disciples, *You shall know the truth, and the truth shall make you free* (John 8:32), He was referring not only to an intellectual assent to the truth, but also to the application of truth in the most basic issues of life: our goals, our motives, and our sense of self-worth. Unfortunately, many of us give only lip-service to the powerful truths of the Scriptures without allowing them to affect the basis of our self-esteem in a radical way. Instead, we continue to seek our security and purpose from worldly sources: personal success, status, beauty, wealth, and the approval of others. These rewards may fulfill us for a short time, but they soon lead us to a sense of urgency to succeed and be approved again.

To meet these compelling needs, we drive ourselves to achieve, doing virtually anything to make people happy with us, and spend countless hours and dollars trying to look "just right." Often, we avoid situations and people where the risks of failure and rejection are high. It's a rat race that can't be won by simply running faster. We need to get off of this hopeless treadmill, and learn to apply the foundational truths that can motivate us to live for Christ rather than for the approval of other people.

Christ's death paid the penalty for our sins, and His resurrection gives us new life, new goals, and new hope. He has given us complete security and challenging purpose. These are not based on our abilities, but on His grace and the power of His Spirit. Yes, Christ wants us to be zealous and ambitious, but not about our success or status. If we understand His forgiveness and acceptance, we will pursue the right things—Christ and His cause—and we will be free to enjoy His love.

The principles and insights in this book have been gleaned from years of counseling experience and also, from the writings of many psychologists and Bible teachers. I am indebted to their scholarship and wisdom.

This book focuses on how our thoughts affect our emotional, relational and spiritual development. It is not a textbook for professionals. Instead, the goal of this book is to enable a wide range of people to apply the Scriptures specifically and deeply to real issues in their lives. The scope of this material does not include some factors. For instance, some emotional problems have a physiological source (e.g. schizophrenia, learning disabilities, chemical imbalances, etc.); some disorders have their roots in emotional and relational pain but are complicated by physiological symptoms (e.g. chronic fatigue, mood swings, weight loss or gain, migraines, etc.). These factors should certainly be addressed by a competent, qualified physician or psychotherapist if they exist.

This condensed version from the revised and expanded version of *The Search for Significance* book/workbook covers chapters 1 through 7 from the book and four false belief tests from the workbook. The response from those who have read *The Search for Significance* and used its workbook has been overwhelming. It is my prayer that the Lord will use these materials to convince you of His love, forgiveness, and purposes for your life.

> *For the love of Christ controls us, having concluded this,*
> *that one died for all, therefore all died;*
> *and He died for all, that they who live should no longer*
> *live for themselves, but for Him who died and rose again on*
> *their behalf.*

2 Cor. 5:14–15

One
Turning on the Light

Tim Woodall is a young regional sales representative for a company that manufactures building materials. He travels by car, covering a large section of East Texas as he visits building supply stores in the many small towns there.

Almost a year ago, after his last appointment in the day, Tim decided to drive home instead of spending another night in a motel. At about midnight, driving down a lonely, two-lane country highway, he dozed off. His car ran off the road, hit an embankment, and flipped over.

Tim was dazed, and when he moved, seemed to hurt all over. He managed to struggle out of his car, and then lay on the grass trying to grasp what had happened to him. *I'm okay*, he kept telling himself. *It's really not that bad.*

About forty-five minutes later, Tim, barely conscious, heard the sound of an approaching car. He tried to raise himself up, but it was useless; he was too weak. The car zoomed past, and then braked. Bob and Natalie Johnson were driving through the night from El Paso, Texas, to Montgomery, Alabama, to visit their daughter. In the moonlight, Natalie had spotted the overturned car from the corner of her eye. Now, her husband backed down the road and pulled over onto the shoulder. Beyond their headlights, they could clearly see the wrecked car, and lying next to it, Tim.

Tim lay in a pool of blood. Beneath the light, the Johnsons discovered that his head and arm were badly cut, and as they tried to help him to his feet, realized that his left leg was probably fractured.

Seeing his own blood-stained shirt; the dirt, wet beside him; and the concern on the Johnsons' faces, Tim began to shake uncontrollably, suddenly aware that he was badly hurt. He was, in fact, slowly bleeding to death, but due to shock, wasn't fully able to comprehend the extent of his wounds.

The Johnsons lifted Tim into their car and sped him toward the county hospital, where his cuts were stitched and his fractured leg put into a splint. This would be replaced with a cast when the swelling went down.

If the Johnsons hadn't been driving to Alabama that night; if Natalie had been looking another way; if the headlights of their car hadn't enabled them to find Tim in the darkness, he might have died.

This story illustrates a reality in many of our lives: We are hurt, emotionally, relationally, and spiritually, but because we aren't aware of the extent of our wounds, we can't take steps toward healing and health. Our problem is not stupidity, but a lack of objectivity. Because of this, we fail to see the reality of pain, hurt, and anger in our lives.

A college student was considered "the life of the party." She was intelligent, witty, and sociable, but when she was alone, she experienced deep loneliness and seething resentment.

A businessman who, as a child, was neglected by his ambitious father thought, *If I can just get that promotion, then I'll be happy. Success is what really counts in life!* He got many promotions and raises because he was driven to perform well, but happiness continued to elude him.

A housewife with three children painfully wonders, *Why is it that I don't feel close to my husband?* Having grown up with an alcoholic father and a demanding mother, this woman has never felt lovable, and so isn't able to receive her husband's love.

An articulate pastor speaks powerfully about the unconditional love and grace of God, yet he is plagued by guilt. He is driven to succeed in his public ministry, but is passive and withdrawn around his family. He has never understood how to apply his own teaching to *his* life and relationships.

We all have experienced the inability to be objective about our experiences, thoughts, and behavior in different circumstances. This objective "light" didn't begin to penetrate my own life until shortly after I had entered the business world. Before that time, whenever I felt the pain of rejection, the sting of sarcasm, or anything less than the complete approval of others, I tried to shrug it off. I reasoned that because of my status as a Christian, I should exude an attitude of happiness and contentment in all things. When something didn't go the way I'd hoped or planned it would, I simply told myself it didn't really matter. Though I was able to fool myself in these instances, my gloomy countenance told those who were closest to me another story.

On one such occasion, a good friend of mine inquired about what was wrong. "You seem troubled," he said. "Is anything bothering you?"

"Me? No, I'm fine."

"You don't seem fine to me," he persisted. "You're acting as though you might be depressed about something."

I stuck to my time-tested text. "No, really, I *am* fine. I guess I've just been a little pressured lately."

The truth was that an idea I'd presented in a business meeting the week before had been challenged and later, shot down. I didn't think it really mattered at first, but after hearing my friend's remarks, I began to wonder if I were being honest with myself.

Several weeks later, I phoned this friend to thank him for confronting me about my behavior. I briefly told him about the business meeting and said, "Realizing I was hurt because my idea was rejected has enabled me to be honest with the Lord about my feelings and begin working through them."

"I'm sorry about what happened," he said, "but I appreciate your honesty, and think it's great that you're doing something constructive with a difficult situation."

Over time, I began to confide in this friend about other problems I encountered. He helped me a great deal. At times, he would say, "Here's how I'd feel in your situation. I'd be angry because.... Do *you* feel angry?" Or, "I'd be hurt because.... Do *you* feel hurt?"

In the light of his honesty and love, and through the gracious work of the Holy Spirit, I began to be honest with myself and with God. The tough exterior I had developed started cracking, and I began to experience the pain I had neither wanted nor allowed myself to feel. This was hardly pleasant, but acknowledging the presence of hurt in my life was my first step toward finding comfort.

Why do some of us lack objectivity? Why can't we see the reality of our lives? Why are we afraid to "turn on the lights"?

There are a number of answers to these questions, and they vary for each person. Perhaps we think that our situations are "normal," that experiencing loneliness, hurt, and anger is really all there is to life. Perhaps we want to be "good Christians," and believing that *good* Christians don't have problems or feelings like ours, we deny the existence of our painful emotions. Perhaps our lack of objectivity is a learned response from childhood. All of us desperately want our parents to be loving and supportive. If ours aren't (or weren't), we may protect our concept of them by blaming ourselves for their lack of love, and deny that we have been hurt by their behavior.

Human beings develop elaborate defense mechanisms to block pain and gain significance. We suppress emotions; we are compulsive perfectionists; we drive ourselves to succeed, or withdraw and become passive; we attack people who hurt us; we punish ourselves when we fail; we try to say clever things to be accepted; we help people so that we will be appreciated; and we say and do countless other things.

A sense of need usually propels us to look for an alternative. We may have the courage to examine ourselves and may desperately want to change, but may be unsure of how and where to start. We may refuse to look honestly within for fear of what we'll find, or we may be afraid that even if we can discover what's wrong, nothing can help us.

It is difficult—if not impossible—to turn on the light of objectivity by ourselves. We need guidance from the Holy Spirit, as well as the honesty, love, and encouragement of at least one other person who's willing to help us. Even then, we may become depressed as we begin to discover the effects of our wounds. Some of us have deep emotional and spiritual scars resulting from the neglect, abuse, and manipulation that often accompany living in a dysfunctional family (alcoholism, drug abuse, divorce, absent father or mother, excessive anger, verbal and/or physical abuse, etc.), but all of us bear the effects of our own sinful nature and the imperfections of others.

Whether your hurts are deep or relatively mild, it is wise to be honest about them in the context of affirming relationships so that healing can begin.

Many of us mistakenly believe that God doesn't want us to be honest about our lives. We think that He will be upset with us if we tell Him how we really feel. But the Scriptures tell us that God does not want us to be superficial—in our relationship with Him, with others, or in our own lives. David wrote, *Surely you desire truth in the inner parts; you teach me wisdom in the inmost place* (Ps. 51:6, NIV).

The Lord desires truth and honesty at the deepest level, and wants us to experience His love, forgiveness, and power in *all* areas of our lives. Experiencing His love does not mean that all of our thoughts, emotions, and behaviors will be pleasant and pure. It means that we can be *real*, feeling pain and joy, love and anger, confidence and confusion.

The Psalms give us tremendous insight about what it means to be honest with the Lord. David and other psalmists wrote and spoke honestly about the full range of their responses to situations. For example, David expressed his anger with the Lord because he felt abandoned by Him:

> *I say to God my Rock, "Why have you forgotten me?*
> *Why must I go about mourning, oppressed by the enemy?"*
> Ps. 42:9-10, NIV

At times, David was very angry with others, and expressed that anger to the Lord in terms that reveal the depth of his feelings:

> *Break the teeth in their mouths, O God; tear out, O Lord, the fangs of the lions!*
> *Let them vanish like water that flows away; when they draw the bow, let their arrows be blunted.*
> *Like a slug melting away as it moves along, like a stillborn child, may they not see the sun.*
> *Before your pots can feel the heat of the thorns—whether they be green or dry—the wicked will be swept away.*
>
> Ps. 58:6-9, NIV

David wrote of his despair about difficult situations:

> *My heart is in anguish within me; the terrors of death assail me.*
> *Fear and trembling have beset me; horror has overwhelmed me.*
>
> Ps. 55:4-5, NIV

And he communicated his despair to the Lord:

> *Why do you hide your face and forget our misery and oppression?*
> *We are brought down to the dust; our bodies cling to the ground.*
>
> Ps. 44:24-25, NIV

Sometimes, he was confused:

> *How long, O Lord? Will you forget me forever? How long will you hide your face from me?*

> *How long must I wrestle with my thoughts and every day have sorrow in my heart?*
>
> Ps. 13:1-2, NIV

Sometimes, David communicated his love for the Lord:

> *As the deer pants for streams of water, so my soul pants for you, O God.*
> *My soul thirsts for God, for the living God. When can I go and meet with God?*
>
> Ps. 42:1-2, NIV

At times, David trusted in the Lord:

> *The Lord is my light and my salvation—whom shall I fear? The Lord is the stronghold of my life—of whom shall I be afraid?*
> *When evil men advance against me to devour my flesh, when my enemies and my foes attack me, they will stumble and fall.*
> *Though an army besiege me, my heart will not fear; though war break out against me, even then I will be confident.*
>
> Ps. 27:1-3, NIV

At other times, he was filled with praise for God:

> *I will exalt you, my God the King; I will praise your name for ever and ever.*
> *Every day I will praise you and extol your name for ever and ever.*
> *Great is the Lord and most worthy of praise; his greatness no one can fathom.*
>
> Ps. 145:1-3, NIV

These passages demonstrate that God, who spoke of David as a man after His own heart, wants us to be open and honest with Him about *all* of our emotions, not just the pleasant ones.

Some people can read passages like these and begin moving toward healing and health rather quickly. Others, however, may read and study, go to seminars and meetings—they may even be in relationships where they are loved and encouraged—but they may not see substantive change in their lives and patterns of behavior. One reason for this spiritual and emotional inertia is a sense of hopelessness. For various reasons (family background, past experiences, poor modeling), we may have negative presumptions which determine our receptivity to love and truth. In some cases, God's light may have revealed our pain and wall of defenses, but it may not yet have penetrated to our deepest thoughts and beliefs about ourselves. These beliefs may not be clearly articulated, but often reflect misperceptions such as these:

- *God doesn't really care about me.*
- *I am an unlovable, worthless person. Nobody will ever love me.*
- *I'll never be able to change.*
- *I've been a failure all my life. I guess I'll always be a failure.*
- *If people really knew me, they wouldn't like me.*

When the light of love and honesty shines on thoughts of hopelessness, it is often very painful. We begin to admit that we really do feel negatively about ourselves—and have for a long time. But God's love, expressed through His people, and woven into our lives by His Spirit and His Word can, over a period of time, bring healing even to our deepest wounds and instill within us an appropriate sense of self-worth.

The purpose of this book is to provide clear, biblical instruction about the basis of your self-worth by helping you:

1. Identify and understand the nature of man's search for significance.

2. Recognize and challenge inadequate answers.
3. Apply God's solutions to *your* search for significance.

This is a process which we will examine throughout the following pages. At this point, simply ask the Lord to give you the courage to be honest. Give Him permission to shine His Spirit's light on your thoughts, feelings, and actions. You may be surprised by additional pain as you realize the extent of your wounds, but our experience of healing can only be as deep as our awareness of the need for it. This takes the power of God's light. Ask Him to turn on the light.

Author's Note:

With the proliferation of books on both secular and Christian psychology, it is helpful to get a perspective of the biblical principles taught in *The Search for Significance.*

Some Christian counselors and authors observe the pain caused by low self-esteem, and try to inflate a person's ego so that he will feel better about himself. Often, this is simply "positive mental attitude" material in Christian lingo.

Some authors and counselors abhor the shallowness of this "let's all feel good about ourselves" approach, but their response takes them to the other extreme. They camp on Christ's teaching that we should hate our lives in order to be His disciples, excluding the abundant and clear teaching of Christ's love, forgiveness, and acceptance. This harsh, out-of-balance approach may be stimulating to someone who is very secure in Christ, but it is devastating to most of us.

A healthy, positive self-esteem is not attained by "feel good" superficiality. On the other hand, a Christ-centered view of ourselves is not detrimental to true discipleship; it is the result of understanding and applying the truths of the Scriptures. A proper view of God and of ourselves enables us to love, obey, and honor Christ with full hearts. Paul wrote, *For through the grace given to me I say to every man among you not to think more highly of himself than he ought to think; but to think so as to have sound judgment* . . . (Rom. 12:3). This sound judgment is not based on either pop psychology or spiritual masochism. Sound judgment is based squarely on God's truth. *The Search for Significance* is designed to present His truth clearly.

Two
Our Search for Significance

Relatively few of us experience the blend of contentment and godly intensity that God desires for each person. From life's outset, we find ourselves on the prowl, searching to satisfy some inner, unexplained yearning. Our hunger causes us to search for people who will love us. Our desire for acceptance pressures us to perform for the praise of others. We strive for success, driving our minds and bodies harder and farther, hoping that because of our sweat and sacrifice, others will appreciate us more.

But the man or woman who lives only for the love and attention of others is never satisfied—at least, not for long. Despite our efforts, we will never find lasting, fulfilling peace if we have to continually prove ourselves to others. Our desire to be loved and accepted is a symptom of a deeper need—the need that often governs our behavior and is the primary source of our emotional pain. Often unrecognized, this is our need for self-worth.

The case of Mark and Beth aptly demonstrates this great need. During their final semester at Cornell University, Mark and Beth fell in love. Beth's eyes sparkled, her walk had that certain lightness, and she found it difficult to concentrate on her studies. As she and Mark gazed into each other's eyes, Beth saw the special affection she had always desired. She felt that her need to feel valued and loved would be fulfilled through their relationship. Likewise, Mark was encouraged and motivated by

Beth's acceptance and admiration of him. With her support, Mark thought he could boldly begin a successful career after graduation.

The summer after they graduated from Cornell, Mark and Beth married, believing their love would provide them both with a permanent sense of self-worth. Unfortunately, they were depending on each other to fill a void that could only be filled by their Creator. Each expected the other to always be loving, accepting, and forgiving, but soon both were disillusioned and even felt betrayed by the other. As the years passed, affirmation was replaced by sarcasm and ridicule. Because each had anticipated that the other would consistently provide love and acceptance, each failure to do so was another brick in their wall of hurt and separation. Recently, Mark and Beth celebrated their tenth wedding anniversary. Sadly, although they had shared ten years with each other, they had experienced very little true, unconditional love for each other. Their search for self-worth and significance ended in despair.

Another example illustrates how the promise of fulfillment through success is an empty one, often resulting in tragic consequences for ourselves and those around us:

Brad and Lisa had been married for twelve years. Brad was a successful lawyer, and Lisa was a homemaker extensively involved in church activities. Their two sons, six-year-old Kyle and eight-year-old David, were well-behaved boys. Although their family appeared to be a model of perfection to those around them, Brad and Lisa were beginning to experience some real problems. True, Brad's law practice was flourishing, but at the expense of Lisa and the boys. He arrived home later and later each evening, and often spent the weekend locked in his office. Brad was driven to succeed, believing that satisfaction and contentment were always just one more trial victory away. But each success gave him only temporary fulfillment. *Maybe the next one....*

Brad would not allow anything to interfere with his success, not even the needs of his family. At first, Lisa seemed to understand. She knew Brad's work was important and hated to protest when he was so busy. Not wanting to burden him, she began to feel guilty for talking to him about family problems. But as the weeks turned into months, and Brad remained obsessed with his work, Lisa became resentful. Even though it was painful, she could overlook her own needs, but the boys needed their father. The family never had time to be together any more, and Brad's promises had begun to sound hollow. "When this big case is over, the pressure will be off," he'd say, but there was always another case. Brad was continually solving other people's problems, but never those of his own family. Realizing that she and the boys weren't important to him, Lisa became bitter and depressed.

As Brad and Lisa's problems persisted, they became obvious to others. Friends began asking Lisa what was wrong. Finding it difficult at first to be honest about the situation, Lisa eventually shared her feelings. She was both hurt and surprised by the glib responses she received from well-meaning but insensitive friends. "Just trust the Lord," one said. Another close friend advised, "You shouldn't have any problems, Lisa. You're a Christian. With God's help, you can work it out."

Like falling on a jagged rock, these comments hurt deeply. Lisa began to doubt herself and wonder if she were capable of building a successful marriage and family. Feeling like a failure, she reasoned that perhaps she deserved a broken marriage; perhaps her problems with Brad were her fault and God was punishing her for her sins.

Confused and frustrated, both Brad and Lisa were searching for significance in their own ways—Brad in his success as an attorney, and Lisa in her success as a wife and mother. Their lives began to reflect that strange combination of hopelessness and compulsion. Sadly, neither Brad nor Lisa realized that their search should both begin and end with God's Word.

In the Scriptures, God supplies the essentials for discovering our true significance and worth. The first two chapters of Genesis recount man's creation, revealing man's intended purpose (to honor God) and man's value (that he is a special creation of God). John 10:10 also reminds us of how much God treasures His creation, in that Christ came so that man might experience "abundant life." However, as Christians, we need to realize that this abundant life is lived in a real world filled with pain, rejection, and failure. Therefore, experiencing the abundant life God intends for us does not mean that our lives will be problem-free. On the contrary, life itself is a series of problems that often act as obstacles to our search for significance, and the abundant life is the experience of God's love, forgiveness, and power in the midst of these problems. The Scriptures warn us that we live within a warfare that can destroy our faith, lower our self-esteem, and lead us into depression. In his letter to the Ephesians, Paul instructs us to put on the armor of God so that we can be equipped for spiritual battle. However, it often seems that unsuspecting believers are the last to know this battle is occurring, and that Christ has ultimately won the war. They are surprised and confused by difficulties, thinking that the Christian life is a playground, not a battlefield.

As Christians, our fulfillment in this life depends not on our skills to avoid life's problems, but on our ability to apply God's specific solutions to those problems. An accurate understanding of God's truth is the first step toward discovering our significance and worth. Unfortunately, many of us have been exposed to inadequate teaching from both religious and secular sources concerning our self-worth. As a result, we may have a distorted self-perception, and may be experiencing hopelessness rather than the rich and meaningful life God intends for us.

Christian psychologist, Lawrence J. Crabb, Jr., describes our need for self-esteem this way: "The basic personal need of each person is to regard himself as a worthwhile human being." And, according to William Glasser, "Everyone aspires to have a happy, successful, pleasurable belief in himself."

Some secular psychologists focus on self-worth with a goal of simply feeling good about ourselves. A biblical self-concept, however, goes far beyond that limited perspective. It is an accurate perception of ourselves, God, and others based on the truths of God's Word. An accurate, biblical self-concept contains both strength and humility, both sorrow over sin and joy about forgiveness, a deep sense of our need for God's grace and a deep sense of the reality of God's grace.

Whether labeled "self-esteem" or "self-worth," the feeling of significance is crucial to man's emotional, spiritual, and social stability, and is the driving element within the human spirit. Understanding this single need opens the door to understanding our actions and attitudes.

What a waste to attempt to change behavior without truly understanding the driving needs that cause such behavior! Yet, millions of people spend a lifetime searching for love, acceptance, and success without understanding the need that compels them. We must understand that this hunger for self-worth is God-given and can only be satisfied by Him. Our value is not dependent on our ability to earn the fickle acceptance of people, but rather, its true source is the love and acceptance of God. He created us. He alone knows how to fulfill *all* of our needs.

In order to fully understand the provisions that God has made for our self-worth, we must look back to man's beginning—to the first man and woman, and their search for significance.

Three
The Origin of the Search

The Old Testament depicts the original incident of sin and the Fall of Man:

> *When the woman saw that the tree was good for food, and that it was a delight to the eyes, and that the tree was desirable to make one wise, she took from its fruit and ate; and she gave also to her husband with her, and he ate.*
>
> *Then the eyes of both of them were opened, and they knew that they were naked; and they sewed fig leaves together and made themselves loin coverings.*
>
> Gen. 3:6-7

To understand the devastating effects of this event properly, we need to examine the nature of man before sin caused him to lose his security and significance.

The first created man lived in unclouded, intimate fellowship with God. He was secure and free. In all of God's creation, no creature compared to him. Indeed, Adam was a magnificent creation, complete and perfect in the image of God, designed to reign over all the earth (Gen. 1:26-28). Adam's purpose was to reflect the glory of God. Through man, God wanted to demonstrate His holiness (Ps. 99:3-5); love and patience (1 Cor. 13:4); forbearance (1 Cor. 13:7); wisdom (James 3:13, 17); comfort (2 Cor. 1:3-4); forgiveness (Heb. 10:17); faithfulness (Ps. 89:1, 2, 5, 8); and grace (Ps. 111:4). Through his intellect, free will, and emotions, man was to be the showcase for God's glorious character.

Adam was, therefore, a very important creation to God. To meet his needs for companionship and understanding, God created a woman for Adam and gave her to him as his wife. In keeping with their perfect character, God placed Adam and Eve in a perfect environment—a lush, beautiful garden where the Creator Himself provided for their physical needs. Adam and Eve had the challenge and responsibility of supervising this paradise of vegetation and animal life. To satisfy Adam and Eve's spiritual needs, God visited them and talked with them personally. Adam and Eve were perfect in body, mind, and spirit.

Like Adam and Eve, Satan also was created in perfection. At the time of his creation, his name was Lucifer, which means "morning star." He was an angel of the highest rank, created to glorify God. He was clothed with beauty and power, and was allowed to serve in the presence of God. Sadly, Lucifer's pride caused him to rebel against God, and he was cast from heaven with a third of the angels (Is. 14:12-15). When he appeared to Adam and Eve in the garden, it was in the form of a serpent, *more crafty than any beast of the field which the Lord God had made* (Gen. 3:1).

Adam had been given authority over the earth, but if he, like Lucifer, rebelled against God, he would lose both his authority and perfection. He would become a slave to Satan and to sin (Rom. 6:17), and a child of God's wrath (Eph. 2:3). Therefore, destroying man was Satan's way to reign on earth and, he apparently thought, to thwart God's glorious plan for man.

To accomplish his goal, Satan began by deceiving Eve, who fell to the temptation. Eve ate of the tree of the knowledge of good and evil, believing it would make her wise and like God. Adam, however, was not deceived. He deliberately chose to forsake the love and security of God and follow Eve in sin. Paul explained this fact to Timothy:

> *And it was not Adam who was deceived, but the woman*
> *being quite deceived, fell into transgression.*
>
> 1 Tim. 2:14

In doing this, Adam not only lost the glory God had intended for mankind, but he also forfeited his close communion and fellowship with God. Adam's deliberate rebellion also aided Satan's purpose, giving him power and authority on earth. From that moment on, all history led to a single hill outside of Jerusalem, where God appointed a Savior to pay the penalty for man's sin of rebellion.

Though we justly deserve the wrath of God because of that deliberate rebellion (our attempts to find security and purpose apart from Him), His Son became our substitute, experienced the wrath our rebellion deserves, and paid the penalty for our sins. Christ's death is the most overwhelming evidence of God's love for us. Because Christ paid for our sins, our relationship with God has been restored, and we are able to partake of His nature and character, to commune with Him, and to reflect His love to all the world.

Spread the good news! Man is not lost forever! God has not given up on us! He has bought us out of slavery to sin by the payment of Christ's death on the cross. Satan's rule can be broken and we can reign with Christ. We can be restored to the security and significance for which we have been created—not simply in eternity, but here and now as well.

We must never forget that God wants His children to bear His image and to rule with Him. Adam's sin has had tragic consequences, but through God's plan of redemption, we can still have the unspeakable privilege of relating to Him. God has provided the solution, but the question is this: Will we accept Christ's death as the payment for our sins and discover the powerful implications of our salvation, or will we continue to follow Satan's lies and deceptions?

Perhaps you are unsure of your relationship with God and need to deal conclusively with this choice now. We cannot pay for our sins; Christ has already done this for us as a free gift. Paul wrote to the Ephesian Christians:

> *For by grace* (unmerited favor) *you have been saved* (rescued from spiritual death—hell) *through faith* (trust); *and that not of yourselves, it is the gift of God;*
> *not as a result of works, that no one should boast.*
>
> Eph. 2:8-9

Are you trusting in your own abilities to earn acceptance with God, or are you trusting in the death of Christ to pay for your sins, and the resurrection of Christ to give you new life? Take a moment to reflect on this question: On a scale of 0-100 percent, how sure are you that you would spend eternity with God if you died today? An answer of less than 100 percent may indicate that you are trusting, at least in part, in yourself. You may be thinking, *Isn't it arrogant to say that I am 100 percent sure?* Indeed, it would be arrogance if you were trusting in yourself—your abilities, your actions, and good deeds—to earn your salvation. However, if you are no longer trusting in your own efforts, but in the all-sufficient payment of Christ, then 100 percent certainty is a response of humility and thankfulness, not arrogance.

Reflect on a second question: If you were to die today and stand before God, and He were to ask you, "Why should I let you into heaven?" what would you tell Him? Would you mention your abilities, church attendance, kindness to others, Christian service, abstinence from a particular sin, or some other good deed? Paul wrote to Titus:

> *But when the kindness of God our Savior and His love for mankind appeared,*
> *He saved us, not on the basis of deeds which we have done in righteousness, but according to His mercy. . . .*
>
> Titus 3:4-5

We must give up our own efforts to achieve righteousness, and instead believe that Christ's death and resurrection alone are sufficient to pay for our sin and separation from God.

Perhaps you have intellectually believed that Jesus Christ lived 2,000 years ago, performed miracles, died on the cross, and was raised from the dead. Perhaps you have even felt close to God at times in your life. But biblical faith is more than intellectual assent or warm emotions.

Consider the analogy of a wedding: An engaged couple may intellectually know they want to marry each other, and probably feel very close to one another, but until they willfully say, "I do" to each other, they are not married. Many people are at this point in their relationship with Christ. They need to say, *I do* to Him.

If there is any question about whether you have conclusively accepted Christ's substitutionary death to pay for the wrath you deserve for your sins, take some time to think about the two questions we have examined, and reflect on His love and forgiveness. Then, respond by trusting in Christ and accepting His payment for your sins. You can use this prayer to express your faith:

> *Lord Jesus, I need You. I want You to be my Savior and Lord. I accept Your death on the cross as the complete payment for my sins. Thank You for forgiving me and for giving me new life. Help me to grow in my understanding of Your love and power so that my life will bring honor to You. Amen.*

The moment you trust Christ, many wonderful things happen to you:

All your sins are forgiven: past, present, and future (Col. 2:13-14).
You become a child of God (John 1:12; Rom. 8:15).
You receive eternal life (John 5:24).
You are delivered from Satan's domain and transferred into the kingdom of Christ (Col. 1:13).

Christ comes to dwell within you (Col. 1:27; Rev. 3:20).
You become a new creation (2 Cor. 5:17).
You are declared righteous by God (2 Cor. 5:21).
You enter into a love relationship with God (1 John 4:9-11).
You are accepted by God (Col. 1:19-22).

Think on the implications of these truths in your life. Then, thank God for His wonderful grace and experience *the love of Christ which surpasses knowledge* (Eph. 3:19).

Some people may ask, "How does baptism relate to this conversion experience?" Water baptism is a visible demonstration of a believer's internal conversion to Christ. It enables the believer to identify himself with Christ in his culture. The act of baptism symbolizes his being dead, buried, and raised with Christ. In the early church and in some countries today, this identification is a dramatic statement of being severed from the world and being bonded to the body of Christ. In our society, it is still an important step of obedience as we identify ourselves publicly with Christ and His people. (For a sample of passages on Spirit baptism and water baptism, see Acts 8:26-39; Rom. 6:1-4, and 1 Cor. 12:13.)

Four

The Saving Solution vs. Satan's Snare

Satan, the father of lies, twists and distorts the truth so that his deceptions appear to be more reasonable and attractive than the truth. Notice how Satan snared Eve. He told her:

> *For God knows that in the day you eat from it your eyes will be opened, and you will be like God, knowing good and evil.*

Gen. 3:5

Here, Satan directly questioned God's truthfulness, implying that Eve could have greater significance apart from God, and that eating the forbidden fruit would reveal hidden knowledge, enabling her to know good from evil like God Himself.

Being deceived, Eve traded God's truth for the serpent's lie. She ate the forbidden fruit. Then, Adam followed her in sinful rebellion against God, and he, too, ate the forbidden fruit. One of the tragic implications of this event is that man lost his secure status with God and began to struggle with feelings of arrogance, inadequacy, and despair, valuing the opinions of others more than the truth of God. This has robbed man of his true self-worth and has put him on a continual, but fruitless, search for significance through his success and the approval of others.

In one form or another, Satan's lie still thrives today. For example, humanism, the central philosophy of our schools and society, teaches that man is above all else, that he alone is the center of meaning. Teaching that man has meaning totally apart from God, humanism leaves morality, justice, and behavior to the discretion of "enlightened" man and encourages people to worship man and nature rather than God. Living without God's divine truth, humanity sinks lower and lower in depravity, blindly following a philosophy that intends to heighten the dignity of man, but which instead lowers him to the level of animals. Rather than a spiritual and emotional being, man has been classified as merely natural phenomena of time plus chance, no greater than rocks, animals, or clouds. The Apostle Paul described this foolish and demeaning perspective of man in Rom. 1:20-25:

> *For since the creation of the world His invisible attributes, His eternal power and divine nature, have been clearly seen, being understood through what has been made, so that they are without excuse.*
>
> *For even though they knew God, they did not honor Him as God, or give thanks; but they became futile in their speculations, and their foolish heart was darkened.*
>
> *Professing to be wise, they became fools,*
>
> *and exchanged the glory of the incorruptible God for an image in the form of corruptible man and of birds and four-footed animals and crawling creatures.*
>
> *Therefore God gave them over in the lusts of their hearts to impurity, that their bodies might be dishonored among them.*
>
> *For they exchanged the truth of God for a lie, and worshiped and served the creature rather than the Creator, who is blessed forever. Amen.*

In the beginning, God declared that man was created to reign with Him; however, man rejected God's truth and chose instead to believe Satan's lie. Today, man continues to reject God's truth and offer of

salvation through Jesus Christ. He choos
and the opinions of others to give him a s
Scriptures clearly teach that apart from Ch
condemned to an eternity in hell.

Since the Fall, man has often failed to
himself. Instead, he has looked to others to n
self-worth. *I am what others say I am*, he has r
in their opinions of me.

Isn't it amazing that we turn to others who have a perspective as
limited and darkened as our own to discover our worth! Rather than
relying on God's steady, uplifting reassurance of who we are, we depend
on others who base our worth on our ability to meet their standards.

Because our performance and ability to please others so dominates
our search for significance, we have difficulty recognizing the distinction
between our real identity and the way we behave, a realization crucial to
understanding our true worth. Our true value is not based on our behavior
or the approval of others, but on what God's Word says is true of us.

Our behavior is often a reflection of our beliefs about who we are.
It is usually consistent with what we think to be true about ourselves (Prov.
23:7). If we base our worth solidly on the truths of God's Word, then our
behavior will often reflect His love, grace, and power. But if we base our
worth on our abilities or the fickle approval of others, then our behavior
will reflect the insecurity, fear, and anger that comes from such instability.

Though we usually behave in ways that are consistent with our
beliefs, at times, our actions may contradict them. For example, we may
believe that we are generous and gracious, when we are actually very
selfish. Sometimes, our behavior changes what we believe about ourselves.
If, for instance, we succeed in a task at which we initially believed we
would fail, our confidence may begin to grow and expand to other areas of
our lives. Our feelings, behavior, and beliefs all interact to shape our lives.

Our home environment plays a central role in forming our beliefs
and emotions, and these can have a powerful impact on our outlook and
behavior.

truth is evident in the case of Scott. Scott grew up in a home out praise, discouraged by his parents whenever he attempted nything new and challenging. After twenty years of hearing, "You'll never be able to do anything, Scott, so don't even try," he believed it himself. Neither Scott nor his parents could later understand why he had flunked out of college and was continually shuffling from one job to another, never able to achieve success. Believing he was doing the best he could do, but suspecting he would always fail, Scott consistently performed according to his self-perception.

Separated from God and His Word, people have only their abilities and the opinions of others on which to base their worth, and the circumstances around them ultimately control the way they feel about themselves.

Take the case of Stacy, a young girl who became pregnant when she was seventeen. Stacy gave her baby up for adoption, and only her family and a few close friends knew of the incident. Several years later, Stacy fell in love with a compassionate man named Ron and married him. Fearing his reaction, she didn't tell Ron about the baby.

Over the years, Stacy concealed her guilt and grief until the pressure finally became so overwhelming that she admitted the entire episode to him.

Surprisingly, Ron did not respond in anger. He understood the agony his wife had carried for so many years and loved her in spite of her past. It was Stacy who could not cope at this point. Unable to accept Ron's forgiveness, and knowing she had failed according to society's standards, Stacy felt unworthy of his love. Stacy refused to forgive herself and chose to leave her husband.

In this case, Stacy fell victim to one of Satan's most effective lies: *Those who fail are unworthy of love and deserve to be blamed and condemned.* Because she failed in her own eyes, Stacy's perception of herself was detrimentally affected.

Each of us has probably failed badly at some point in our lives. Perhaps some particular sin or weakness has caused us to feel condemned and unworthy of love. Without the hope and healing that God can provide, our evaluation of ourselves will eventually lead to despair.

In spite of Adam and Eve's sin, God's plan is to bring man back to the destiny for which he was originally created—to bear His image. To accomplish this, God gives a new nature to all who believe in Christ. This new nature is able to reflect God's character and rule His creation. In Luke 10:19, Jesus spoke of the authority of this new nature when He said, *Behold, I have given you authority to tread upon serpents and scorpions, and over all the power of the enemy, and nothing shall injure you.*

Satan, however, continues to deceive people, including many Christians, into believing that the basis of their worth is their performance and their ability to please others. The equation below reflects Satan's lie:

SELF-WORTH = PERFORMANCE + OTHERS' OPINIONS

Can we overcome Satan's deception and reject this basis of our self-worth? Can we trust God's complete acceptance of us as His sons and daughters, and allow Him to free us from our dependency on success and the approval of others? Rejecting Satan's lie and accepting God's evaluation of us leads to a renewed hope, joy, and purpose in life.

We all have compelling, God-given needs for love, acceptance, and purpose, and most of us will go to virtually any lengths to meet those needs. Many of us have become masters at "playing the game" to be successful and win the approval of others. Some of us, however, have failed and have experienced the pain of disapproval so often that we have given up and have withdrawn into a shell of hurt, numbness, or depression. In both cases, we are living by the deception that our worth is based on our performance and others' opinions—some of us are simply more adept at playing this game than others.

Our attempts to meet our needs for success and approval fall into two broad categories: compulsiveness and withdrawal.

Some people expend extra effort, work extra hours, and try to say just the right thing to achieve success and please those around them. These people may have a compelling desire to be in control of every situation. They are perfectionists. If a job isn't done perfectly, if they aren't dressed just right, if they aren't considered "the best" by their peers, then they work harder until they achieve that coveted status. And woe to the poor soul who gets in their way! Whoever doesn't contribute to their success and acclaim is a threat to their self-esteem—an unacceptable threat. They may be very personable and have a lot of "friends," but the goal of these relationships may not be to give encouragement and love; it may be to manipulate others to contribute to their success. That may sound harsh, but people who are driven to succeed will often use practically everything and everybody to meet that need.

The other broad category is withdrawal. Those who manifest this behavior usually try to avoid failure and disapproval by avoiding risks. They won't volunteer for the jobs that offer much risk of failure. They gravitate toward people who are comforting and kind, skirting relationships that might demand vulnerability, and consequently, the risk of rejection. They may appear to be easygoing, but inside they are usually running from every potential situation or relationship that might not succeed.

Obviously, these are two broad categories. Most of us exhibit some combination of the two behaviors, willing to take risks and work hard in the areas where we feel sure of success, but avoiding the people and situations that may bring rejection and failure.

Rob and Kathy had dated for three years. Kathy was a perfectionist. Her clothes, her hair, her work, her car...and her boyfriend had to be perfect. Rob, a good-natured, fun-loving fellow, was not as concerned with such details. Predictably, the more intense Kathy became about having everything and everybody "just right," the more passive and easygoing Rob became. This spiral of intensity and passivity continued until Rob and Kathy hit rock bottom.

After several weeks of counseling, Kathy saw that her perfectionism came from a misplaced base of security: her performance instead of Christ. But Rob said that he didn't have a problem with performance. He certainly didn't have a compelling drive to succeed, and he didn't pressure people around him to "get their act together." In the midst of these explanations, I asked, "But Rob, what about your tendency to withdraw? Why do you think you do that?" It still didn't compute.

Finally, after several months, Rob understood. He based his security on his performance just as much as Kathy did, but he handled it differently. She became more compulsive to have things "just right," while he withdrew to avoid failure. Both slowly began to recognize the root of their problems, and through months of encouragement and honest interaction, they started believing that their worth is secure in Christ. Today, Kathy is less intense about her performance, and Rob doesn't run from failure as much as he used to. They are learning to channel their intensity toward the right things: Christ and His kingdom.

When we base our security on success and others' opinions, we become dependent on our abilities to perform and please others. We develop a *have-to* mentality: *I have to do well on this exam (or my security as a "good student" will be threatened); I have to make that deal (or it will mean that my boss will think I am a failure); My father (or mother, spouse, or friend) has to appreciate me and be happy with my decisions (because I cannot cope with his disapproval).*

Our self-esteem and view of God are usually a mirror of our parents' attitudes toward us. Those who are loved and affirmed by their parents tend to have a fairly healthy self-concept, and usually find it easy to believe that God is loving and powerful. Those whose parents have been neglectful, manipulative, or condemning usually seem to feel that they have to earn a sense of worth, and that God is aloof, demanding, and/or cruel.

Our parents are our models of the character of God. When we do not have that fundamental sense of feeling lovable and protected by them, then we tend to base our self-worth on how well we perform and please others, instead of on what the sovereign God of the universe, our all-wise, omniscient Savior says of us.

We do not *have to* be successful or *have to* be pleasing to others to have a healthy sense of self-esteem and worth. That worth has freely and conclusively been given to us by God. Failure and/or the disapproval of others can't take it away! Therefore, we can conclude, *It would be nice to be approved by my parents* (or whomever), *but if they don't approve of me, I'm still loved and accepted by God.* Do you see the difference? The *have-to* mentality is sheer slavery to performance and the opinions of others, but we are secure and free in Christ. We don't *have to* have success or anyone else's approval. Of course, it would be nice to have success and approval, but the point is clear: Christ is the source of our security; Christ is the basis of our worth; Christ is the only One who promises and never fails.

The transition from the slavery and compulsion of a *have-to* mentality to the freedom and strength of a *want-to* motivation is a process. Bondage to such thinking is often deeply rooted in our personalities, patterns of behavior, and ways of relating to other people. These patterns of thinking, feeling, and responding—learned over time—flow as naturally as the course of rainwater in a dry desert riverbed. Changing them requires time, the encouragement of others, the truth and application of God's Word, and the power of God's Spirit.

This book is dedicated to the process of understanding, applying, and experiencing the foundational truths of God's Word. In the remaining chapters, we will examine the process of hope and healing. We will also identify four specific false beliefs generated by Satan's deception. In addition, we will discover God's gracious, effective, and permanent solution to our search for significance.

Five

The Process of Hope and Healing

In the first chapter of this book, we saw that Tim Woodall had a car accident late in the evening on a lonely country highway in East Texas. Tim was broken and bleeding, but because he was in shock, he was completely unaware of the extent of his injuries.

Aided by their car's headlights, the Johnsons realized that Tim needed immediate attention, and took him to the nearest hospital. Tim stayed there for three days. The doctors waited for the swelling in his leg to go down before putting it in a cast, and then kept him for observation, knowing that the blow to his head might have caused a concussion.

Tim's wife took him home from the hospital, and after a week or so, the pain in his leg began to subside, and the stitches were removed from his head and arm. Tim wasn't sure which was worse: limping around on his crutches, or looking at himself in the mirror. The nurse had shaved a portion of his scalp for the stitches, and his new appearance took some getting used to for everyone—but especially for Tim.

Three months later, Tim's cast was removed, and a new hairstyle gave him a far more presentable appearance. It was several more months before he was able to build strength back into his leg muscles again, but after awhile, the only marks left from the accident were the scars, which weren't readily noticeable.

Tim's rehabilitation was a process. It wasn't spontaneous. His injuries required attention and expert care. Emotional, spiritual, and relational healing is a process, too. It doesn't happen overnight, but it can happen.

Several elements are required for emotional healing. These are not consecutive steps to be accomplished one after the other. They are ingredients which promote healing by working together simultaneously over a period of time. These elements are honesty; affirming relationships; right thinking; the Holy Spirit's power, strength, and wisdom; and time. If any of these is missing, then the healing process will be hindered, if not completely stifled.

Let's examine these ingredients:

Honesty

As we noted in chapter 1, we can apply and experience healing only to the depth that we are aware of our need for it. If we are completely unaware of our need, we won't seek a solution. If we are only superficially aware of our need and honest about it, we may only seek (and find) superficial remedies. But if we are encouraged to be honest about our painful needs at a deeper level, then we can experience the power of healing and comfort at that level.

Affirming Relationships

People seldom have the objectivity and the courage to be honest about reality in their lives without some affirmation from others. The love, strength, and honesty we find in other people are tangible expressions of those traits that are characteristic of God. A friend, a small group, a pastor, or a counselor who won't be frustrated by our slow progress—and who won't give us quick and easy solutions—is a valuable find! (Of course, it is always wise to use discretion and discernment regarding what and with whom we share. The act of sharing is a responsibility.) Pray that God will provide a person or group of persons with whom you can be open and honest, who can objectively listen to you and share with you, and who will encourage you to make real, rather than superficial progress.

Right Thinking

Many of us are unaware of what we really believe about God and about ourselves. We often say what we don't mean, and mean what we don't say. God's Word is our guide. It is truly *a lamp for our feet and a light for our path* (Ps. 119:105). And yet, we often experience difficulty in applying scriptural concepts to our lives because of the elaborate array of defenses we have structured over the years to protect ourselves. It is important to understand that Scripture can be used to identify and attack these defensive barriers, enabling us to experience an open and honest relationship with God:

> *For the word of God is living and active and sharper than any two-edged sword, and piercing as far as the division of soul and spirit, of both joints and marrow, and able to judge the thoughts and intentions of the heart.*
>
> *And there is no creature hidden from His sight, but all things are open and laid bare to the eyes of Him with whom we have to do.*
>
> Heb. 4:12-13

The Holy Spirit

Deep, spiritual healing requires giving attention to the whole man, to his emotional, relational, physical, and spiritual needs. The Holy Spirit is given by God to communicate His love, light, forgiveness, and power to our deepest needs. This spiritual aspect of healing is perhaps the most fundamental, because our view of God (and subsequent relationship with Him) can determine the quality and degree of health we experience in every other area of our lives.

Some of us believe that the Holy Spirit's ministry is characterized only by positive, pleasant emotions like love and joy. However, one of the miracles of the Holy Spirit's work is that of producing honesty and courage in our lives as we grapple with the reality of pain. He is the Spirit of truth, not denial, and He enables us to experience each element of the healing process as He gives us wisdom, strength, and encouragement through God's Word and other people.

Time

If we were computers, solutions to our problems would be produced in microseconds. People, however, don't change that quickly. The agrarian metaphors given in the Scriptures depict *seasons* of planting, weeding, watering, growth, and harvesting. Farmers don't expect to plant seeds in the morning and harvest their crops that afternoon. Seeds must go through a complete cycle of growth, receiving plenty of attention in the process, before they mature. In this age of instant coffee, microwave dinners, and instant banking, we tend to assume that spiritual, emotional, and relational health will be instantaneous. These unrealistic expectations only cause discouragement and disappointment.

Although this book's primary focus is on the cognitive, or right-thinking, aspect of our spiritual growth, we need to remember that all of these elements are required to produce growth and health. Our growth will be stunted and superficial if we don't give proper emphasis to honesty about our emotions, affirming relationships, right thinking promoted through biblical study and application, the ministry of the Holy Spirit, and time.

Some of us seem to respond to this environment of growth very quickly; others, after a few weeks or months; and still others, never at all. Why the difference? Why are some of us able to apply principles of growth so much more readily that others?

Again, differing factors will produce a variety of responses from different people. Those who respond quickly may not be as wounded as others, or they may already be in an environment which has prepared them for relatively rapid growth.

Some of us are in situations where one or more elements of growth are in some way missing or lacking. We may be trying to deal with our difficulties alone. We may be depending on a rigid structure of discipline for positive change, instead of blending a healthy combination of our responsibility with the Holy Spirit's enabling power. We may be expecting too much too soon, and may be experiencing disappointment with our slow results. Some of us may, in fact, be ready to quit the growth process entirely.

Those of us who can't seem to get the light turned on have the greatest difficulty in beginning this process. We can't see our problems. We may recognize that something is wrong, but can't pinpoint exactly what. Or, our defense mechanisms of denial may be so strong that we're unable to see any needs in our lives at all.

A young man asked me, "What about people from very stable backgrounds? They don't wrestle with the difficulties you're talking about, do they?"

"All of us have a fallen, sinful nature," I responded. "Because of that, we all wrestle to some degree with the fears of failure and rejection, and with feelings of inadequacy, guilt, and shame. Those from stable, loving families are usually better able to determine what their difficulties are, and be honest about them, than those who are shackled by the defense mechanisms that are often developed in dysfunctional families.

"Those from abusive, manipulative, or neglectful families have far more to overcome than those from a healthier home environment," I explained. "Alcoholism, divorce, sexual abuse, physical abuse, workaholism, drug abuse, and other major family disorders leave deep wounds. Many people from backgrounds like these have suppressed their intense hurt and anger for so long that they are simply out of touch with the reality in their lives. Therefore, just as a broken arm requires more time, attention, and therapy for healing than does a small abrasion, people suffering from deep emotional, spiritual, and relational injuries need more time, attention, love, and encouragement than those with more minor wounds. Though the process for recovery may take longer, enjoying health in these areas is still possible if all the elements of healing are applied over its duration."

Another person asked, "Why doesn't just understanding these issues work? Why isn't knowledge enough to produce change?"

"Man is a relational, physical, emotional, and spiritual being," I said. "We develop and learn and grow best in an environment of honesty, love, and affirmation, where all aspects of our nature are given the encouragement to heal."

A woman asked me, "What do I need to do to begin seeing some results?"

"Put yourself in an environment of growth, which includes all the elements of honesty, affirming relationships, right thinking, the ministry of the Holy Spirit, and time. I can't tell you how or when growth will come—but I know that it will come if you are patient and persistent."

A businessman asked, "Why do I not see much change in my life?"

After talking with him for awhile, three issues surfaced which can be common to many of us: First, this gentleman had advanced significantly in his profession by performing well and pleasing people. Although he had received promotions, raises, prestige, and comfort, he still wasn't happy. Yet, it was difficult for him to consider living by a pattern of behavior other than that which had seemingly brought him so far.

In addition, this man was afraid of how he might respond to the generosity of God's love and freedom. He feared that he would either abuse God's grace or be so changed by it that some of his friends and business associates might make fun of him and ultimately reject him.

Finally, he feared that if he did respond wholeheartedly to God's love, the Lord might test his faith by making his life miserable. "I couldn't stand that," he told me. "My life is painful now, but at least I'm used to it. If I surrender completely to God, my life might get totally out of control."

These and many other reasons make the process of spiritual, relational, emotional, and mental health elusive to many people. But again, honesty is our starting point. When we are willing to be open about our thoughts
and fears, we generally find that others have thought and felt much the same way.

Our growth toward wholeness and maturity is a journey which won't be completed until we join the Lord in heaven. The Apostle Paul understood this, and saw himself as being in the middle of this process. He wrote to the Philippian believers:

> *Not that I have already obtained it, or have already become perfect, but I press on in order that I may lay hold of that for which I was laid hold of by Christ Jesus.*
>
> Phil. 3:12

If Paul, the foremost missionary and writer of much of the New Testament, saw himself as being "in the process," we can be encouraged to continue in the process toward change as well. It will help to have reasonable expectations about our progress. Sometimes, we will experience flashes of insight and spurts of growth, but the process of healing and renewal will more often be slow and methodical. Our emotions, too, may occasionally be very pleasant and positive, but when God's light shines on another area of hurt in our lives, we will likely experience another round of pain and anger. Remember that healing can only continue as we put ourselves in an environment characterized by honesty, affirming relationships, right thinking, the Holy Spirit's love and power, and time.

Introduction to Chapters Six, Seven, Eight, and Nine

It is often helpful to see a general outline when attempting to grasp new concepts. In the next four chapters, we will examine four false beliefs resulting from Satan's deceptions with some of the consequences that accompany these beliefs. Finally, we will examine God's specific solution for our false belief system, and apply this through some practical exercises.

Remember that the specific consequences of false beliefs and resulting actions vary from person to person, depending on family background, personality traits, other relationships, and many other factors. Likewise, the application of biblical truths will vary according to the perception of the individual, the degree of his or her emotional, spiritual, and relational health, and the process by which the cognitive, relational, spiritual, and emotional elements are incorporated into his or her life. All of this takes time, but health and hope are worth it!

⁎ The chart on the following pages provides an overview of the next four chapters:

Chapter	False Beliefs
Six The Performance Trap	*I must meet certain standards in order to feel good about myself.*
Seven Approval Addict	*I must be approved (accepted) by certain others to feel good about myself.*
Eight The Blame Game	*Those who fail are unworthy of love and deserve to be punished.*
Nine Shame	*I am what I am. I cannot change. I am hopeless.*

Consequences	God's Answer
The fear of failure; perfectionism; driven to succeed; manipulating others to achieve success; withdrawal from risks.	**Justification** *Justification means that God has not only forgiven me of my sins, but has also granted me the righteousness of Christ. Because of justification, I bear Christ's righteousness and am, therefore, fully pleasing to the Father* (Rom. 5:1).
The fear of rejection; attempting to please others at any cost; overly sensitive to criticism; withdrawing from others to avoid disapproval.	**Reconcilation** *Reconciliation means that although I was at one time hostile toward God and alienated from Him, I am now forgiven and have been brought into an intimate relationship with Him. Consequently, I am totally accepted by God* (Col. 1:21-22).
The fear of punishment; punishing others; blaming others for personal failure; withdrawal from God and others; driven to avoid failure.	**Propitiation** *Propitiation means that Christ satisfied God's wrath by His death on the cross; therefore, I am deeply loved by God* (1 John 4:9-11).
Feelings of shame, hopelessness, inferiority; passivity; loss of creativity; isolation; withdrawal from others.	**Regeneration** *Regeneration means that I am a new creation in Christ* (John 3:3-6).

One man asked me, "Why do you include only *four* false beliefs? Doesn't Satan also use many others?"

"Yes," I replied, "he uses an endless variety of deceptions to confuse and distort the truth of God; yet, in my study of the Scriptures and through my interaction with people, these four seem to represent the central issues we struggle with in our desire for significance."

"Can a person experience more than one false belief in a given situation?" he asked.

"Yes, of course," I said. "Many of life's circumstances reveal that we are basing our response to a situation on more than one of Satan's lies. Usually, however, close examination will reveal that one may be more foundational. For example, I may be afraid to fail, but the real reason I fear failure could be that I'm afraid that my failure might result in the disapproval of others."

We will explore the interrelationship of misconceptions after we've identified the false beliefs in the following chapters.

Six
The Performance Trap

Most of us are unaware of how thoroughly Satan has deceived us. He has led us blindly down a path of destruction, captives of our inability to meet our standards consistently, and slaves of low self-esteem. Satan has shackled us in chains that keep us from experiencing the love, freedom, and purposes of Christ.

In Col. 2:8, Paul warns:

> *See to it that no one takes you captive through philosophy and empty deception, according to the tradition of men, according to the elementary principles of the world, rather than according to Christ.*

Indeed, we've reached a true mark of maturity when we begin testing the deceitful thoughts of our minds against the Word of God. We no longer have to live by our fleshly thoughts; we have the mind of Christ (1 Cor. 2:16). Through His Spirit, we can challenge the indoctrinations and traditions that have long held us in guilt and condemnation. We can then replace those deceptions with the powerful truths of the Scriptures.

A primary deception all of us tend to believe is that success will bring fulfillment and happiness. Again and again, we've tried to measure up, thinking that if we could meet certain standards, we would feel good about ourselves. But again and again, we've failed and have felt miserable. Even if we succeed on a fairly regular basis, occasional failure may be so devastating that it dominates our perception of ourselves.

Consciously or unconsciously, all of us have experienced this feeling that we must meet certain arbitrary standards to attain self-worth. Failure to do so threatens our security and significance. Such a threat, real or perceived, results in a fear of failure. At that point, we are accepting the false belief: *I must meet certain standards in order to feel good about myself.* When we believe this about ourselves, Satan's distortion of truth is often reflected in our attitudes and behavior.

Because of our unique personalities, we each react very differently to this deception. As we saw in a previous chapter, some of us respond by becoming slaves to perfectionism—driving ourselves incessantly toward attaining goals.

Perfectionists can be quite vulnerable to serious mood disorders, and often anticipate rejection when they believe they haven't met the standards they are trying so hard to attain. Therefore, perfectionists tend to react defensively to criticism and demand to be in control of most situations they encounter. Because they are usually more competent than most, perfectionists see nothing wrong with their compulsions. "I just like to see things done well," they claim. There is certainly nothing inherently wrong with doing things well; the problem is that perfectionists usually base their self-worth on their ability to accomplish a goal. Therefore, failure is a threat and is totally unacceptable to them.

Karen, a wife, mother, and civic leader, seemed ideal to everyone who knew her. She was a perfectionist. Her house looked perfect, her kids were spotless, and her skills as president of the Ladies' Auxiliary were superb. In each area of her life, Karen was always in charge, always successful. However, one step out of the pattern she had set could lead to a tremendous uproar. When others failed to comply with her every demand, her condemnation was quick and cruel.

One day, her husband decided that he couldn't stand any more of Karen's hypercritical behavior. He wanted an understanding wife to talk and share with, not an egocentric, self-driven perfectionist. Friends later could not understand why he chose to leave his seemingly perfect wife.

Like Karen, many high achievers are driven beyond healthy limitations. Rarely able to relax and enjoy life, they let their families and relationships suffer as they strive to accomplish often unrealistic goals.

On the other hand, the same false belief *(I must meet certain standards to feel good about myself)* that drives many to perfectionism sends others into a tailspin of despair. They rarely expect to achieve anything or to feel good about themselves. Because of their past failures, they are quick to interpret present failures as an accurate reflection of their worthlessness. Fearing more failure, they often become despondent and stop trying.

Finally, the pressure of having to meet self-imposed standards in order to feel good about ourselves can result in a rules-dominated life. Individuals caught in this trap often have a set of rules for most of life's situations, and continually focus their attention on their performance and ability to adhere to their schedule. Brent, for example, made a daily list of what he could accomplish if everything went perfectly. He was always a little tense because he wanted to use every moment effectively to reach his goals. If things didn't go well, or if someone took too much of his time, Brent got angry. Efficient, effective use of time was his way of attaining fulfillment, but he was miserable. He was constantly driven to do more, but his best was never enough to satisfy him.

Brent believed that accomplishing goals and making efficient use of his time were what the Lord wanted him to do. Due to stress, he occasionally thought that *something* wasn't quite right, but his solution was to try harder, make even better use of his time, and be even more regimented in his adherence to self-imposed rules.

Brent's focus was misdirected. The focus of the Christian life should be on Christ, not on self-imposed regulations. Our experience of Christ's lordship is dependent on our moment-by-moment attention to His instruction, not our own regimented schedule.

As these cases demonstrate, the false belief, *I must meet certain standards in order to feel good about myself,* results in a fear of failure. How affected are you by this belief? Take the following test to determine how strongly you fear failure.

FEAR OF FAILURE TEST

Read each of the following statements; then, from the top of the test, choose the term which best describes your response. Put the number above that term in the blank beside each statement.

1	2	3	4	5	6	7
Always	Very Often	Often	Sometimes	Seldom	Very Seldom	Never

____ 1. Because of fear, I often avoid participating in certain activities.

____ 2. When I sense that I might experience failure in some important area, I become nervous and anxious.

____ 3. I worry.

____ 4. I have unexplained anxiety.

____ 5. I am a perfectionist.

____ 6. I am compelled to justify my mistakes.

____ 7. There are certain areas in which I feel I *must* succeed.

____ 8. I become depressed when I fail.

____ 9. I become angry with people who interfere with my attempts to succeed, and as a result, make me appear incompetent.

____ 10. I am self-critical.

____ Total (Add up the numbers you have placed in the blanks.

Interpretation of Score
If your score is...

57-70

God has apparently given you a very strong appreciation for His love and unconditional acceptance. You seem to be freed from the fear of failure that plagues most people. (Some people who score this high are either greatly deceived, or have become callous to their emotions as a way to suppress pain.)

47-56

The fear of failure controls your responses rarely, or only in certain situations. Again, the only major exceptions are those who are not honest with themselves.

37-46

When you experience emotional problems, they may relate to a sense of failure or to some form of criticism. Upon reflection, you will probably relate many of your previous decisions to this fear. Many of your future decisions will also be affected by the fear of failure unless you take direct action to overcome it.

27-36

The fear of failure forms a general backdrop to your life. There are probably few days that you are not affected in some way by this fear. Unfortunately, this robs you of the joy and peace your salvation is meant to bring.

0-26

Experiences of failure dominate your memory, and have probably resulted in a great deal of depression. These problems will remain until some definitive action is taken. In other words, this condition will not simply disappear; time alone cannot heal your pain. You need to experience deep healing in your self-concept, in your relationship with God, and in your relationships with others.

EFFECTS OF THE FEAR OF FAILURE

The fear of failure can affect our lives in many ways. The following list is not an exhaustive discussion of its resulting problems, nor are these problems explained completely by the fear of failure. However, recognizing and confronting the fear of failure in each of these experiences could result in dramatic changes.

Perfectionism

Again, one of the most common symptoms of the fear of failure is perfectionism, an unwillingness to fail. This tendency suffocates joy and creativity. Because any failure is perceived as a threat to our self-esteem, we develop a propensity to focus our attention on the one area in which we failed rather than those in which we did well. Areas where we often tend to be perfectionistic include work, punctuality, house-cleaning, our appearance, hobbies and skills—practically anything and everything!

Perfectionists often appear to be highly motivated, but their motivations usually come from a desperate attempt to avoid the low self-esteem they experience when they fail.

Avoiding Risks

Another very common result of the fear of failure is a willingness to be involved in only those activities that can be done well. New, challenging activities are avoided because the risk of failure is too great. Avoiding risks may seem comfortable, but it severely limits the scope of our creativity, self-expression, and service to God.

Anger, Resentment

When we fail, when others contribute to our failure, or when we are injured or insulted in some way, anger is a normal response. Feeling angry isn't wrong. In fact, the Apostle Paul encouraged the Ephesians to *be angry*, but quickly followed that encouragement with the admonition to avoid expressing anger in a sinful, or hurtful, way (Eph. 4:26).

Unfortunately, rather than using our anger constructively, many of us either vent our fury without a thought of its result, or we suppress it. Repressed anger eventually leads to retaliatory outbursts, deep and seething resentment, and/or depression.

Anxiety and Fear

Failure is often the source of self-condemnation and the disapproval of others, both of which are severe blows to a self-worth based on personal success and approval. If failure is great enough or occurs often enough, it can harden into a negative self-concept in which we will expect to fail at virtually every endeavor. This negative self-concept perpetuates itself and leads to a downward spiral of anxiety about our performance and fear of disapproval from others.

Pride

When we base our self-worth on our performance and are successful, we often develop an inflated view of ourselves: pride. Some of us may persist in this self-exaltation through any and all circumstances; for most of us, however, this sense of self-esteem lasts only until our next failure (or risk of failure). The self-confidence that most of us try to portray is only a facade to hide our fear of failure and insecurity.

Depression

Depression is generally a result of anger turned inward and/or a deep sense of loss. Experiencing failure and fearing subsequent failure can lead to deep depression. Once depressed, many become emotionally numb and passive in their actions, believing there is no hope for change. Occasionally, depressed people may also exhibit outbursts of anger resulting from failure. Generally, depression is the body's way of blocking psychological pain by numbing physical and emotional functions.

Low Motivation

Much of what is known as low motivation or laziness is better understood as hopelessness. If people believe they will fail, they have no reason to exert any effort. The pain they endure for their passivity seems relatively minor and acceptable compared to the agony of genuinely trying and failing.

Sexual Dysfunction

The emotional trauma caused by failure can cause disturbances in sexual activity. Then, rather than experience the pain of failing sexually, many tend to avoid sex altogether.

Chemical Dependency

Many people attempt to ease their pain and fear of failure by using drugs or alcohol. Those who abuse alcohol often do so with the false notion that it will increase their level of performance, thus enhancing their attempts at being successful. Alcohol, however, is a depressant, and actually decreases the user's performance ability.

Stimulants also are often used to increase productivity. Users of these drugs are likely to consume larger doses on an increasingly regular basis until they are addicted. This is because natural physiological processes deplete bodily resources during drug binges, so that when users come down from the chemical's "high" effect, they crash and are unable to rise to any occasion without it.

Taking a drink—like playing tennis, jogging, seeing a movie, or reading a book—can be a refreshing means of temporary escape. The problem is that chemical substances are addictive, and often, easily abused. For those who find themselves trapped by chemical dependency, what may have begun as a pleasurable means of temporary escape, or an effort to remove pressures to perform, ends with the despair of realizing an inability to cope without the substance. This pain-pleasure cycle continues, slowly draining the life from its victim.

Because of their euphoric effect, alcohol or drugs may give us an illusion that we are "on top of the world." But success, or the idea of success, regardless of how it is achieved, cannot dictate our sense of self-esteem.

In the case of chemical substances, cocaine users provide a clear example of this truth. A major reason for cocaine's popularity is its ability to produce feelings of greater self-esteem. However, it is interesting to note that a number of highly successful people use this drug. If success truly provided a greater sense of self-esteem, these people would probably not be in the market for the drug in the first place.

As long as we operate according to Satan's lies, we are susceptible to the fear of failure. Our personal experience of this fear is determined by the difference between our performance standards and our ability to meet those standards.

Although we all will continue to experience the fear of failure to some degree, we must realize that as Christians, we have the power provided by the Holy Spirit to lay aside deceptive ways of thinking, and be renewed in our minds by the truth of God's Word (Rom. 12:2; Eph. 4:21-25). For our benefit, God often allows us to experience circumstances which will enable us to recognize our blind adherence to Satan's deceptions. Many times, these circumstances seem very negative, but through them, we can learn valuable, life-changing truths. In Ps. 107:33-36, we see a poetic example of this:

> *He changes rivers into a wilderness, and springs of water into a thirsty ground;*
> *A fruitful land into a salt waste, because of the wickedness of those who dwell in it.*
> *He changes a wilderness into a pool of water, and a dry land into springs of water;*
> *And there He makes the hungry to dwell, so that they may establish an inhabited city.*

Has your fruitful land become a salt waste? Maybe God is trying to get your attention to teach you a tremendously important lesson: that success or failure is not the basis of your self-worth. Maybe the only way you can learn this lesson is by experiencing the pain of failure. In His great love, God leads us through experiences that are difficult but essential to our growth and development.

The more sensitive you become to the fear of failure and the problems it may cause, the more you will understand your own behavior as well as that of others.

GOD'S ANSWER: JUSTIFICATION

If we base our self-worth on our ability to meet standards, we will try to compensate, either by avoiding risks, or by trying to succeed no matter what the cost. Either way, failure looms as a constant enemy.

As I reflect on my life, I recall being especially fearful of failure during my teenage years. This fear was apparent in many areas of my life, but particularly in athletics.

Because I was, from an early age, taller than most children, many perceived that I would be a basketball player. I practiced a lot during that time, and became a very skilled player. In the process, I learned that I could do many things on the court in practice, or while playing with friends, that I would never even attempt to try during a game, when the pressure was intense. I was afraid of failure, and that fear prevented me from doing many things in basketball which I had the ability to do.

The same fear, I now realize, has prevented me from attempting achievement in several other areas of my life. Although God has enabled me to conquer this fear on many occasions, there are still times when I struggle with the risk of failing. This may be surprising to some who have known me and have thought of me as being successful. Yet, those who have experienced great success know that making an important achievement is often followed by the fear of losing that attainment.

Success truly does not reduce the amount of fear we experience in our lives. In fact, success often causes our fears to escalate because we perceive that we have more to lose.

Thankfully, God has a solution for the fear of failure! He has given us a secure self-worth totally apart from our ability to perform. We have been *justified*, placed in right standing before God through Christ's death on the cross, which paid for our sins. But God didn't stop with our forgiveness; He also granted us the very righteousness of Christ (2 Cor. 5:21)!

Visualize two ledgers: on one is a list of all your sins; on the other, the righteousness of Christ. Now exchange your ledger for Christ's. This exemplifies justification—transferring our sin to Christ and His righteousness to us. In 2 Cor. 5:21, Paul wrote:

> *He made Him* (Christ) *who knew no sin to be sin on our behalf, that we might become the righteousness of God in Him.*

I once heard a radio preacher berate his congregation for their hidden sins. He exclaimed, "Don't you know that someday you're going to die and God is going to flash all your sins upon a giant screen in heaven for all the world to see?" How tragically this minister misunderstood God's gracious gift of justification!

Justification carries no guilt with it, and has no memory of past transgressions. Christ paid for all of our sins at the cross—past, present, and future. Hebrews 10:17 says, *And their sins and their lawless deeds I will remember no more.* We are completely forgiven by God!

As marvelous as it is, justification means more than forgiveness of sins. In the same act of love through which God forgave our sin, He also provided for our *righteousness*: the worthiness to stand in God's presence.

By imputing righteousness to us, God attributes Christ's worth to us. The moment we accept Christ, God no longer sees us as condemned sinners. Instead, we are forgiven, we receive Christ's righteousness, and God sees us as creatures who are fully pleasing to Him.

God intended that Adam and his descendants be righteous people, fully experiencing His love and eternal purposes. But sin short-circuited that relationship. God's perfect payment for sin has since satisfied the righteous wrath of God, enabling us to again have that status of righteousness, and to delight in knowing and honoring the Lord.

God desires for those of us who have been redeemed to experience the realities of His redemption. We are forgiven and righteous because of Christ's sacrifice; therefore, we are pleasing to God in spite of our failures. This reality can replace our fear of failure with peace, hope, and joy. Failure need not be a millstone around our necks. Neither success nor failure is the proper basis of our self-worth. Christ alone is the source of our forgiveness, freedom, joy, and purpose.

God works by *fiat*, meaning that He can create something from nothing by simply declaring it into existence. God spoke and the world was formed. He said, "Let there be light," and light appeared. The earth is no longer void because God sovereignly created its abundance.

In the same way, we were condemned, but now we are declared righteous! Romans 5:1 refers to us as *having been justified by faith*, a statement in the past perfect tense. Therefore, if we have trusted in Christ for our salvation, we each can say with certainty, *I am completely forgiven, and am fully pleasing to God.*

Some people have difficulty thinking of themselves as being pleasing to God because they link *pleasing* so strongly with performance. They tend to be displeased with anything short of perfection in themselves, and suspect that God has the same standard.

The point of justification is that we can never achieve perfection on this earth; even our best efforts at self-righteousness are as filthy rags to God (Is. 64:6). Yet, He loves us so much that He appointed His Son to pay for our sins and give to us His own righteousness, His perfect status before God.

This doesn't mean that our actions are irrelevant, and that we can sin all we want. Our sinful actions, words, and attitudes grieve the Lord, but our status as beloved children remains intact. In His love, He disciplines and encourages us to live godly lives—both for our good and for His honor.

The Apostle Paul was so enamored with his forgiveness and righteousness in Christ that he was intensely motivated to please God by his actions and his deeds. In 1 Cor. 6:19-20; 2 Cor. 5:9; Phil. 3:8-11, and in other passages, Paul strongly stated his desire to please, honor, and glorify the One who had made him righteous.

Some people may read these statements and become uneasy, believing that I am discounting the gravity of sin. As you will see, I am not minimizing the destructive nature of sin, but am simply trying to elevate our view of the results of Christ's payment on the cross. Understanding our complete forgiveness and acceptance before God does not promote a casual attitude toward sin. On the contrary, it gives us a greater desire to live for and serve the One who died to free us from sin. Let's look at some strong reasons to obey and serve God with joy:

REASONS FOR OBEDIENCE

The love of God and His acceptance of us is based on grace, His unmerited favor. It is not based on our ability to impress God through our good deeds. But if we are accepted on the basis of His grace and not our deeds, why *should* we obey God? Here are six compelling reasons to obey Him:

Christ's Love

Understanding God's grace compels us to action because love motivates us to please the One who has so freely loved us. When we experience love, we usually respond by seeking to express our love in return. Our obedience to God is an expression of our love for Him (John 14:15, 21), which comes from an understanding of what Christ has accomplished for us on the cross (2 Cor. 5:14-15). We love because He first loved us and clearly demonstrated His love for us at the cross (1 John 4:16-19). Understanding this will highly motivate us to serve Him.

This great motivating factor is missing in many of our lives because we don't really believe that God loves us unconditionally. We expect His love to be conditional, based on our ability to earn it.

Our experience of God's love is based on our perception. If we believe that He is demanding or aloof, we will not be able to receive His love and tenderness. Instead, we will either be afraid of Him or angry with Him. Faulty perceptions of God often prompt us to rebel against Him.

Our image of God is the foundation for all of our motivations. As we grow in our understanding of His unconditional love and acceptance, we will be better able to grasp that His discipline is prompted by care, not cruelty. We will also be increasingly able to perceive the contrast between the joys of living for Christ and the destructive nature of sin. We will be motivated to experience eternal rewards *where neither moth nor rust destroys* (Matt. 6:20). And we will want our lives to bring honor to the One who loves us so much.

Sin Is Destructive

Satan has effectively blinded man to the painful, damaging consequences of sin. The effects of sin are all around us, yet many continue to indulge in the sex, status- and pleasure-seeking, and rampant self-centeredness that cause so much anguish and pain. Satan contradicted God in the Garden when he said, *You surely shall not die!* (Gen. 3:4). Sin is pleasant, but only for a season. Sooner or later, sin will result in some form of destruction.

Sin is destructive in many ways. Emotionally, we may experience the pain of guilt and shame and the fear of failure and punishment. Mentally, we may experience the anguish of flashbacks. We may also expend enormous amounts of time and energy thinking about our sins and rationalizing our guilt. Physically, we may suffer from psychosomatic illnesses or experience pain through physical abuse. Sin may also result in the loss of property, or even the loss of life. Relationally, we can alienate ourselves from others. Spiritually, we grieve the Holy Spirit, lose our testimony, and break our fellowship with God. The painful and destructive effects of sin are so profound that why we don't have an aversion to it is a mystery!

The Father's Discipline

Our loving Father has given us the Holy Spirit to convict us of sin. Conviction is a form of God's discipline, and serves as proof that we have become sons of God (Heb. 12:5-11). It warns us that we are making choices without regard to either God's truth or sin's consequences. If we choose to be unresponsive to the Holy Spirit, our heavenly Father will discipline us in love. Many people do not understand the difference between discipline and punishment. The following chart shows their profound contrasts:

	PUNISHMENT	DISCIPLINE
SOURCE:	God's Wrath	God's Love
PURPOSE:	To Avenge a Wrong	To Correct a Wrong
RELATIONAL RESULT:	Alienation	Reconciliation
PERSONAL RESULT:	Guilt	A Righteous Lifestyle
DIRECTED TOWARD:	Non-Believers	His Children

Jesus bore all the punishment we deserved on the cross; therefore, we no longer need to fear punishment from God for our sins. We should seek to do what is right so that our Father will not have to correct us through discipline, but when we are disciplined, we should remember that God is correcting us in love. This discipline leads us to righteous performance, a reflection of Christ's righteousness in us.

His Commands for Us Are Good

God's commands are given for two good purposes: to protect us from the destructiveness of sin, and to direct us in a life of joy and fruitfulness. We have a wrong perspective if we only view God's commands as restrictions in our lives. Instead, we must realize that His commands are guidelines, given so that we might enjoy life to the fullest.

God's commands should never be considered as a means to gain His approval.

In today's society, we have lost the concept of doing something because it is the right thing to do. Instead, we do things in exchange for some reward or favor, or to avoid punishment. Wouldn't it be novel to do something simply because it is the right thing to do? God's commands are holy, right, and good, and the Holy Spirit gives us the wisdom and strength to keep them. Therefore, since they have value in themselves, we can choose to obey God and follow His commands.

Eternal Rewards

Yet another compelling reason to live for God's glory is the fact that we will be rewarded in heaven for our service to Him. Two passages clearly illustrate this fact:

> *For we must all appear before the judgment seat of Christ, that each one may be recompensed for his deeds in the body, according to what he has done, whether good or bad.*
> 2 Cor. 5:10

> *Now if any man builds upon the foundation with gold, silver, precious stones, wood, hay, straw,*
> *each man's work will become evident; for the day will show it, because it is to be revealed with fire; and the fire itself will test the quality of each man's work.*
> *If any man's work which he has built upon it remains, he shall receive a reward.*
> *If any man's work is burned up, he shall suffer loss; but he himself shall be saved, yet so as through fire.*
> 1 Cor. 3:12-15

Through Christ's payment for us on the cross, we have escaped eternal judgment; however, our actions will be judged at the judgment seat of Christ. There, our performance will be evaluated, and rewards presented for service to God. Rewards will be given for deeds that reflect a desire to honor Christ, but deeds performed in an attempt to earn God's acceptance, earn the approval of others, or meet our own standards will be rejected by God and consumed by fire.

Christ Is Worthy

Our most noble motivation for serving Christ is simply that He is worthy of our love and obedience. The Apostle John recorded his vision of the Lord and his response to His glory:

> *After these things I looked, and behold, a door standing open in heaven, and the first voice which I had heard, like the sound of a trumpet speaking with me, said, "Come up here, and I will show you what must take place after these things."*
>
> *Immediately I was in the Spirit; and behold, a throne was standing in heaven, and One sitting on the throne.*
>
> *And He who was sitting was like a jasper stone and a sardius in appearance; and there was a rainbow around the throne, like an emerald in appearance.*
>
> *And around the throne were twenty-four thrones; and upon the thrones I saw twenty-four elders sitting, clothed in white garments, and golden crowns on their heads. . . .*
>
> *And when the living creatures give glory and honor and thanks to Him who sits on the throne, to Him who lives forever and ever,*
>
> *the twenty-four elders will fall down before Him who sits on the throne, and will worship Him who lives forever and ever, and will cast their crowns before the throne, saying,*
>
> *"Worthy art Thou, our Lord and our God, to receive glory and honor and power; for Thou didst create all things, and because of Thy will they existed, and were created."*
>
> Rev. 4:1-4, 9-11

Christ is worthy of our affection and obedience. There is no other person, no goal, no fame or status, and no material possession that can compare with Him. The more we understand His love and majesty, the more we will praise Him and desire that He be honored at the expense of everything else. Our hearts will reflect the psalmist's perspective:

> *Whom have I in heaven but Thee? And besides Thee, I desire nothing on earth. . . .*
> *But as for me, the nearness of God is my good; I have made the Lord God my refuge, that I may tell of all Thy works.*
>
> Ps. 73:25, 28

A SUMMARY

We obey God because...

1. Christ's love motivates us to live for Him.
2. Sin is destructive and should be avoided.
3. Our Father lovingly disciplines us for wrongdoing.
4. His commands for us are good.
5. We will receive eternal rewards for obedience.
6. He is worthy of our obedience.

Obeying Christ for these reasons is not a self-improvement program. The Holy Spirit gives us encouragement, wisdom, and strength as we grow in our desire to honor the Lord.

A BEGINNING EXERCISE

How can we begin to experience God's freedom from our fear of failure? How can we begin to live in the light of our justification? Reflecting on the following passage of Scripture will help us to get started:

> *For as he thinks within himself, so he is.*
>
> Prov. 23:7

From this passage of Scripture, and from what we know about ourselves, we can draw the following conclusions and applications:

1. Though some of us are more reflective than others, most of us spend a great deal of time thinking about our performance.

2. We have a choice: We can use the same method we have always used to evaluate ourselves and others (Our Self-Worth = Performance + Others' Opinions), or we can adopt God's evaluation (Our Self-Worth = God's Truth About Us).

3. If we want our lives to be what God has designed them to be, then we must use His truth as our standard of evaluation, rather than our own judgment.

4. To accomplish this change in mindset, we need to apply the following action points:

   a) Memorize this statement: *I have great worth apart from my performance because Christ gave His life for me, and therefore, imparted great value to me. I am deeply loved, fully pleasing, totally forgiven, accepted, and complete in Christ.* Repeat this statement to yourself several times each day for two or three weeks.

   b) Each day, tell those in your family whom you know are Christians, "You are deeply loved, fully pleasing, totally forgiven, accepted, and complete in Christ."

5.   As you do this, these truths can begin to positively reinforce your view of yourself, your relationship with God, and your relationships with others.

6.   Failures, both in your own life and in the lives of your family, can be seen as opportunities to apply this biblical value system. The affirmation of God's love and acceptance can be powerful in shaping a healthy self-concept!

God has given us the Bible as a guidebook. By understanding biblical truths, we will be able to identify the deceptions of Satan; then, we can begin to reject these lies and replace them with the eternal truths of God's Word. This process is not easy, but it is essential to our sense of self-worth and our desire to honor Christ.

You have just read a condensed version of the book section for *The Search for Significance*. Many additional topics are covered in the original book/workbook edition. On the next page, I will give you a brief description of what these chapters offer.

In addition to the Fear of Failure Test found in the previous text, there are three more false belief tests in the complete version of *The Search for Significance*. I have included these three tests for you in Appendix 1.

THE SEARCH FOR SIGNIFICANCE

The following additional topics are covered in the complete book.

Approval Addict - Basing our self-worth on what we believe others think of us causes us to become addicted to their approval. An accurate perception of God will help you to experience more of His unconditional love and acceptance.

The Blame Game - Our perception of success and failure is often our primary basis for evaluating ourselves and others. The memorization and application of the truths in this chapter will have profound effects on your life as your mind is slowly transformed by God's Word.

Shame - When we base our self-worth on past failures, dissatisfaction with personal appearance or bad habits, we often believe *I am what I am, I cannot change, I am hopeless.* Because you have been made brand new, complete in Christ, you no longer need to experience the pain of shame.

Obstacles to Growth - The more fully we understand the implications of Christ's sacrifice, the more we will experience the freedom, motivation, and power God intends for us. God's Word is the source of truth: the truth about Christ, the cross, and redemption.

The Holy Spirit: Our Source of Change - Abiding in Christ does not mean deliverance from all of your problems, but it will provide a powerful relationship with the One who is the source of wisdom for difficult decisions, love to encourage you, and strength to help you endure.

Renewing the Mind - Diligent study of God's Word, trust in the Holy Spirit's power to change us, and the encouragement of other believers can produce minds and lives that are healthy, honest, and fruitful for the kingdom of God.

The Weapons of Our Warfare - Simply indentifying the source of our problems will not free us from them. We must use the weapons God has provided to overcome incorrect thoughts, vain imaginations, and distorted beliefs.

Guilt vs. Conviction - Guilt brings depression and despair, but conviction enables us to realize the beauty of God's forgiveness and to experience His love and power.

The Search Concluded - The sovereign Almighty God is able to accomplish far more than we can understand. We can have faith in His greatness, wisdom, and love, even when we don't understand what He is doing. He has freed us to *proclaim the excellencies of Him who has called you out of darkness into His marvelous light* (1 Peter 2:9).

Appendix 1

FEAR OF REJECTION TEST

Read each of the statements below; then, from the top of the test, choose the term which best describes your response. Put the number above that term in the blank beside each statement.

1	2	3	4	5	6	7
Always	Very often	Often	Sometimes	Seldom	Very seldom	Never

_____ 1. I avoid certain people.

_____ 2. When I sense that someone might reject me, I become nervous and anxious.

_____ 3. I am uncomfortable around those who are different from me.

_____ 4. It bothers me when someone is unfriendly to me.

_____ 5. I am basically shy and unsocial.

_____ 6. I am critical of others.

_____ 7. I find myself trying to impress others.

_____ 8. I become depressed when someone criticizes me.

_____ 9. I always try to determine what people think of me.

_____ 10. I don't understand people and what motivates them.

Total (Add up the numbers you have placed in the blanks.)

Interpretation of Score
If your score is . . .

57–70
God has apparently given you a very strong appreciation for His love and unconditional acceptance. You seem to be freed from the fear of rejection that plagues most people. (Some people who score this high are either greatly deceived, or have become callous to their emotions as a way to suppress pain.)

If you or someone you know is suffering from an emotional problem or substance abuse, call 1-800-847-HOPE.

47–56

The fear of rejection controls your responses rarely, or only in certain situations. Again, the only major exceptions are those who are not honest with themselves.

37–46

When you experience emotional problems, they may relate to a sense of rejection. Upon reflection, you will probably relate many of your previous decisions to this fear. Many of your future decisions will also be affected by the fear of rejection unless you take direct action to overcome it.

27–36

The fear of rejection forms a general backdrop to your life. There are probably few days that you are not in some way affected by this fear. Unfortunately, this robs you of the joy and peace your salvation is meant to bring.

0-26

Experiences of rejection dominate your memory and have probably resulted in a great deal of depression. These problems will persist until some definitive action is taken. In other words, this condition will not simply disappear; time alone cannot heal your pain. You need to experience deep healing in your self-concept, in your relationship with God, and in your relationships with others.

For more information about Rapha's treatment programs,
call 1-800-847-HOPE.

FEAR OF PUNISHMENT/PUNISHING OTHERS TEST

Read each of the statements below; then, from the top of the test, choose the term which best describes your response. Put the number above that term in the blank beside each statement.

1	2	3	4	5	6	7
Always	Very often	Often	Sometimes	Seldom	Very seldom	Never

_____ 1. I fear what God might do to me.

_____ 2. After I fail, I worry about God's response.

_____ 3. When I see someone in a difficult situation, I wonder what he or she did to deserve it.

_____ 4. When something goes wrong, I have a tendency to think that God must be punishing me.

_____ 5. I am very hard on myself when I fail.

_____ 6. I find myself wanting to blame people when they fail.

_____ 7. I get angry with God when someone who is immoral or dishonest prospers.

_____ 8. I am compelled to tell others when I see them doing wrong.

_____ 9. I tend to focus on the faults and failures of others.

_____ 10. God seems harsh to me.

Total (Add up the numbers you have placed in the blanks.)

Interpretation of Score
If your score is . . .

57–70
God has apparently given you a very strong appreciation for His love and unconditional acceptance. You seem to be freed from the fear of punishment and the compulsion to punish others that plague most people. (Some people who score this high are either greatly deceived, or have become callous to their emotions as a way to suppress pain.)

If you or someone you know is suffering from an emotional problem or substance abuse, call 1-800-847-HOPE.

47–56

The fear of punishment and the compulsion to punish others control your responses rarely, or only in certain situations. Again, the only major exceptions are those who are not honest with themselves.

37–46

When you experience emotional problems, they may tend to relate to a fear of punishment or to an inner urge to punish others. Upon reflection, you will probably relate many of your previous decisions to this fear. Many of your future decisions will also be affected by the fear of punishment and/or the compulsion to punish others unless you take direct action to overcome these tendencies.

27–36

The fear of punishment forms a general backdrop to your life. There are probably few days that you are not in some way affected by the fear of punishment and the propensity to blame others. Unfortunately, this robs you of the joy and peace your salvation is meant to bring.

0-26

Experiences of punishment dominate your memory and you probably have suffered a great deal of depression as a result of them. These problems will remain until some definitive plan is followed. In other words, this condition will not simply disappear; time alone cannot heal your pain. You need to experience deep healing in your self-concept, in your relationship with God, and in your relationships with others.

SHAME TEST

Read each of the statements below; then, from the top of the test, choose the term which best describes your response. Put the number above that term in the blank beside each statement.

1	2	3	4	5	6	7
Always	Very often	Often	Sometimes	Seldom	Very seldom	Never

_____ 1. I often think about past failures or experiences of rejection.

_____ 2. There are certain things about my past which I cannot recall without experiencing strong, painful emotions (i.e. guilt, shame, anger, fear, etc.).

_____ 3. I seem to make the same mistakes over and over again.

_____ 4. There are certain aspects of my character that I want to change, but I don't believe I can ever successfully do so.

_____ 5. I feel inferior.

_____ 6. There are aspects of my appearance that I cannot accept.

_____ 7. I am generally disgusted with myself.

_____ 8. I feel that certain experiences have basically ruined my life.

_____ 9. I perceive of myself as an immoral person.

_____ 10. I feel that I have lost the opportunity to experience a complete and wonderful life.

Total (Add up the numbers you have placed in the blanks.)

Interpretation of Score
If your score is . . .

57–70
God has apparently given you a very strong appreciation for His love and unconditional acceptance. You seem to be freed from the shame that plagues most people. (Some people who score this high are either greatly deceived, or have become callous to their emotions as a way to suppress pain.)

If you or someone you know is suffering from an emotional problem or substance abuse, call 1-800-847-HOPE.

47–56

Shame controls your responses rarely, or only in certain situations. Again, the only major exceptions are those who are not honest with themselves.

37–46

When you experience emotional problems, they may relate to a sense of shame. Upon reflection, you will probably relate many of your previous decisions to feelings of worthlessness. Many of your future decisions will also be affected by low self-esteem unless you take direct action to overcome it.

27–36

Shame forms a generally negative backdrop to your life. There are probably few days that you are not in some way affected by shame. Unfortunately, this robs you of the joy and peace your salvation is meant to bring.

0-26

Experiences of shame dominate your memory and have probably resulted in a great deal of depression. These problems will persist until some definitive action is taken. In other words, this condition will not simply disappear; time alone cannot heal your pain. You need to experience deep healing in your self-concept, in your relationship with God, and in your relationships with others.

For more information about Rapha's treatment programs,
call 1-800-847-HOPE.

Appendix 2

The Search for Significance
ROBERT S. MCGEE.

Rated #1 in reader satisfaction by a recent NavPress survey, Robert McGee's best seller deals with the foundational principles of biblically-based self-esteem. This book teaches us how to base our self-worth upon the love, forgiveness, and acceptance that comes through Jesus Christ. The truths presented in *The Search for Significance* form the foundational cornerstones that provide the balance of spiritual and clinical therapy in the Rapha Treatment Centers program. These insights are both profoundly biblical and clearly applicable.

Rapha Resources books and materials may be ordered by calling 1-800-460-HOPE. For more information about Rapha's treatment programs, call 1-800-847-HOPE.

22-DAY GUIDED STUDY
for use with *The Search for Significance*

How could I better help people as they study and work through the Search material?

What if brief, daily conversations were printed to help others understand the study for the day, explaining what may be happening—both good and bad?

What if I offered something, such as a visual hook, that would allow them to easily absorb what was being studied that particular day and help them to remember what they have learned?

You can expect this and more in the *22-Day Guided Study* for *The Search for Significance*. The many experiences and insights I've gained in explaining this material to thousands of people adds to the quality of this superb tool. It is especially beneficial for those whose aptitudes require visual learning techniques. Here are some of the areas I have covered in this study:

Acknowledging God as Your Healer
Giving Your Burdens to the Lord
Healing as a Process
Making Godly Choices
How to "Be Angry and Sin Not"
Turning Away From Anger and Grief and Turning Toward God
What God Says About Self-worth
Childhood Patterns and Outcomes
Overcoming Childhood Patterns
The Performance Trap
Obedience
Addiction to Approval
Blame
Shame
Forgiveness

Rapha Resources books and materials may be ordered by calling 1-800-460-HOPE. For more information about Rapha's treatment programs, call 1-800-847-HOPE.

The Search for Significance Devotional

Robert S. McGee.

This is more than a typical book of meditations. Because of the challenges and pressures of today's world, we need a fresh perspective on life, self-esteem, and inner peace.

This 90-day guide has a different topic for each day, reflection questions, and weekly journals to help you apply these devotions to your life.

Rapha Resources books and materials may be ordered by calling 1-800-460-HOPE. For more information about Rapha's treatment programs, call 1-800-847-HOPE.

Father Hunger
ROBERT S. MCGEE.

McGee offers practical insight into the types of fathers we have on earth and our responses to them. *Father Hunger* addresses the child of the severely negligent father as well as the child of a loving yet imperfect father. The author's premise is that our relationship to our earthly father sets a precedent for our relationship to our heavenly Father. His treatment is one that will deeply affect your relationship with God as Abba Father.

Getting Unstuck
ROBERT S. MCGEE & PAT SPRINGLE.

Although recovery is now a well sought after process, many people feel stuck between hurt and healing. The authors offer hope for those who feel trapped in the recovery process. Usually what is hindering complete recovery is their long-buried emotional wounds—wounds that they do not even know exist. Uncovering this unfinished business from the past and seeing how it affects the present can bring the sufferer out of the mud and onto the dry road of wholeness and full recovery. Includes a small group leader's guide.

Rapha Resources books and materials may be ordered by calling 1-800-460-HOPE. For more information about Rapha's treatment programs, call 1-800-847-HOPE.

Codependency:
A Christian Perspective
PAT SPRINGLE.

Divorce, alcoholism, drug abuse, workaholism, and similar problems are destroying the family unit and every member is affected. One of the painful affects is codependency: the compulsion to rescue and control others. A host of corollary characteristics can plague a codependent: being driven to succeed and please people, perfectionism, withdrawal, being easily manipulated, etc.

Codependency will help you recognize these painful results and offers sound, biblical processes that promise hope and healing.

Rapha Resources books and materials may be ordered by calling 1-800-460-HOPE. For more information about Rapha's treatment programs, call 1-800-847-HOPE.

Appendix 3

ROBERT S. McGEE
Founder of Rapha

Dear Reader:

Many factors work together to discourage those who truly need intensive help from receiving that help. Insurance companies who attempt to save money by eliminating unnecessary medical costs, at times show little concern about those who live with intense emotional pain on a daily basis. Politicians have discovered abuses in the health care industry, but instead of true reform, they have adopted media-pleasing reform. They may have indeed reduced some the abuse, but they have done so at the expense of those who truly need help. One might compare this situation to hypothetically eliminating insurance payment for all Cesarean sections only because a small number have been performed without firm medical indication. Finally, historically there have always been the personal barriers; externally and internally we never want to admit the severity of our issues.

As I counseled in a private practice many years ago, I saw numerous people who continued to be trapped in emotional pain, seemingly not able to escape even with the help of once-a-week therapy. Seeing the need for a more intensive type of treatment, I founded Rapha in April 1986, and over 25,000 people have sought and received help since that day. I wish I could tell you that all 25,000 were success stories, but that is not so. However, results of a two-year longitudinal survey completed in 1994 indicate that over 94 percent of the patients responding not only report satisfaction with the program, but a willingness to refer friends and family to Rapha for treatment. Furthermore, over 75 percent of them indicated *their high expectations* for treatment were met. Based on these success stories and others, I believe many thousands have experienced life-long change during their time at Rapha. These folks write to me with their testimonies, come up to greet me after I speak, and openly tell me of their experiences.

For each person who received help at Rapha, there was someone who took the time and effort to encourage that first step. I've often wondered why one person would be an encourager while another would sit idly by and, perhaps, even become a hindrance. I've concluded that those who encourage others have loved enough to understand the pain and hurt of another. They have broken out of the insulated island of loneliness, have touched and been touched by another, and have found the courage to reach out and help.

On the next page, you will read a brief description of the treament programs offered at Rapha. Please look at this prayerfully. Ask God to lead you to those that need His healing touch.

Robert S. McGee

ROBERT S. McGEE
FOUNDER OF RAPHA

RAPHA RESOURCES was independently organized to assist the church and ministry by providing books and resources, education, curriculum, and leadership in Christian counseling and church-led support group activity.

RAPHA TREATMENT CENTERS is a nationally recognized health-care organization that provides psychiatric and chemical dependency programs within a Christ-centered therapeutic perspective. In hospitals and treatment centers located nationwide, Rapha offers a continuum of care for adults and adolescents including acute inpatient, sub-acute, residential, and partial hospitalization; day, evening, and weekend programs; intensive outpatient; an outpatient network, conferences; support group training; books and materials.

If you or someone you know needs help with an emotional problem or substance abuse or for more information about Rapha's services, call

1-800-847-HOPE.

A diagnosis of need for inpatient treatment can be made only by a licensed physician or mental health professional.

Appendix 4

TESTIMONIALS

"Our community is fortunate indeed to have access to the outstanding Christian counseling service Rapha provides. The success of this biblically-based, Christ-centered approach to counseling is further evidence that God's principles work best in every facet of our lives."
Dr. Ed Young
Pastor of Second Baptist Church, Houston, TX

"I appreciate the commitment that Rapha has for the American teenager. Rapha's treatment program is based on a biblical perspective and brings about true healing for emotional needs."
Dawson McAllister
Author and Speaker

"I appreciate the ministry that Rapha is providing to the community as well as to the ministers and churches of the Assemblies of God in South Texas."
Rev. Howard Burroughs
Superintendent, South Texas Assemblies of God, Houston, TX

If you or someone you know is suffering from an emotional problem or substance abuse, call 1-800-847-HOPE.

"I want you to know how grateful I am to God for all you are doing. All of us who are pastors, as we sense the tremendous needs and hurts of people, are thankful for an organization like Rapha."
Dr. Charles Stanley
Pastor of First Baptist Church, Atlanta, GA

"Conferences and seminars presented by Rapha provide both evangelistic opportunities and occasions for spiritual renewal and maturity. People are drawn to these conferences, since they deal with both felt needs and biblical solutions."
Dr. Gene Getz
Senior Pastor of Fellowship Bible Church North, Plano, TX
Director, Center for Church Renewal

"I have been delighted to learn of Rapha's blend of clinical competence and scriptural authority. I believe that Rapha truly lives up to its biblical name through its God-centered caring and healing."
Dr. D. James Kennedy
Sr. Minister of Coral Ridge Presbyterian Church, Fort Lauderdale, FL

"The Christ-centered counseling available at Rapha is a great testimony to the overcoming power of biblical truth when applied to a hurting life. From the abuse recovery programs to codependency counseling and all the other services available through Rapha, they all ring freedom for those bound up in

For more information about Rapha's treatment programs,
call 1-800-847-HOPE.

these areas because they emphasize that truth must not be only learned, but applied, in order to have effectual and lasting change upon a life for the glory of God."

Rev. Tommy Barnett
Pastor of First Assembly of God Church, Phoenix, AZ

"I am so pleased that now there is a Christian organization that has trained, experienced people who, when coupled with their commitment to Jesus Christ, are available to help these hurting people. I truly believe that Rapha is an organization committed to helping the hurting."

Rev. Edward V. Hill
Pastor of Mount Zion Missionary Baptist Church, Los Angeles, CA

If you or someone you know is suffering
from an emotional problem or substance abuse, call

1-800-847-HOPE.

Rapha
TREATMENT ■ CENTERS
Clinically Professional Distinctively Christian

A diagnosis of need for inpatient treatment can be made
only by a licensed physician or mental health professional.

Appendix 5

SEMINARS

We can build our self-worth on our ability to please others, or on the love and forgiveness of Jesus Christ. Here's how you can benefit from a "Search for Significance" seminar!

- Find out how the world's system of self-worth differs from God's plan.

- Learn how our beliefs affect the way we behave.

- Discover how the drive to succeed traps us with a fear of failure and how God can replace that fear.

- Find out how God's power can overcome the fear of rejection.

- Learn how blame and shame keep us from being all God wants us to be.

- Find out how to experience forgiveness for ourselves and others.

- And more!

Search Ministries provides day, weekend, and week-long seminars. For information concerning presently scheduled events or to schedule an event,

call 1-800-460-HOPE.